The history of Soviet Union and how Russia develops nuclear power

Carter Jones

TABLE OF CONTENTS

INTRODUCTION

Nuclear physics research in the Soviet Union dates back to the first decades of the twentieth century. The Radium Laboratory (now known as the Khlopin Radium Institute) was established in 1921 under the auspices of the Russian Academy of Sciences and continues to operate today.

In 1933, the Soviet Union's capital city of Leningrad hosted the inaugural National Conference on Nuclear Physics. Yuri Zeldovich, Yuliy Khariton, and Alexander Leypunsky showed the feasibility of a nuclear fission chain reaction in uranium in 1939, and this was the first time this had been done. In 1940, two researchers at the Radium Institute, Konstantin Petrzhak and Georgiy Flyorov, made the discovery of spontaneous fission of heavy nuclei (without the use of neutron bombardment) for the first time.

The military's 'nuclear program,' which began in the 1940s, gave a huge boost to the expansion of the nuclear sector. On September 28, 1942, the State Defence Committee issued a clandestine directive No. 2352ss on the organization of uranium work, which was kept strictly confidential. A year later, in

1943, Igor Kurchatov was chosen to lead the laboratory that makes measuring instruments for the USSR Academy of Sciences. This lab is now called the National Research Center Kurchatov Institute. On August 20, 1945, a directive was signed designating the Special Committee under the State Defence Committee of the Soviet Union as the controlling body for uranium research and development activities. This date is frequently cited as the official beginning of the nuclear power industry.

Laboratory No. 2's F-1 reactor, which was built in 1946, was the first to achieve a self-sustaining nuclear chain reaction in uranium. Developed in the Soviet Union and Europe, the F-1 nuclear reactor was the world's first nuclear reactor. In 1949, the Soviet Union successfully tested its first nuclear weapon, which was followed by the test of the world's first thermonuclear weapon in 1953, both of which were successful.

With the launch of the Leninsky Komsomolsk, the first Soviet nuclear submarine, the country's 'nuclear shield' contributed to the achievement of a worldwide goal: nuclear parity between the Soviet Union and the United States was believed to have helped prevent the Third World War, while nuclear weapons were transformed into a peaceful containment tool. Beyond defensive capabilities, the Soviet Union placed a strong emphasis on the application of nuclear energy in the civilian sector of the economy. In 1953, the Ministry of Medium Machine-Building was established. In 1957, Efim Slavsky served as the Minister's chief of staff.

A program to develop the nuclear power sector in the Soviet Union was led by academicians Igor Kurchatov and Anatoly Alexandrov, which included widespread use of nuclear energy in power generation, transportation, and other aspects of the national economy. Kurchatov and Alexandrov were both members of the Soviet Academy of Sciences.

The Obninsk Nuclear Power Plant (NPP), the world's first nuclear power plant, began operations in 1954. The Lenin nuclear icebreaker, the world's first nuclear icebreaker, was launched in 1959. The first VVER reactor, with a capacity of 210 MW, was built and installed at the Novovoronezh Nuclear Power Plant in the Soviet Union in 1964. The first RBMK reactor, which had a capacity of 1,000 MW, was built at the Leningrad Nuclear Power Plant in 1974. By the end of the 1980s, the overall nuclear power capacity of the Soviet Union had increased to 37 GW. Soviet atomic scientists laid the groundwork for the future by constructing enormously powerful particle accelerators, nuclear fusion facilities for plasma compression research, and a number of other facilities that are still in use today.

The Chernobyl nuclear disaster in 1986 severely impeded the development of the nuclear power industry. At the same time, this horrifying incident triggered a thorough examination of safety practices, which included the establishment of a safety culture in the workplace. In Russia, the 1990s were a challenging period, but they were also a period of stagnation in the oil and gas sector. However, the nuclear industry,

on the other hand, has survived and maintained its particular research and manufacturing capabilities, in addition to, and perhaps more importantly, its human resource base. During the 2000s, the commissioning of new nuclear power plants (NPPs) continued, with the power unit No. 1 at Rostov NPP and the power unit No. 3 at Kalinin NPP going online in 2001 and 2004, respectively.

Established in 2007, Rosa tom is the Russian State Atomic Energy Corporation. It is a state-owned enterprise. (ROSATOM). The Corporation was given jurisdiction over nuclear weapons by the now-defunct Federal Atomic Energy Administration (the successor to the Soviet Ministry of Medium Machine-Building). ROSATOM began the onerous job of combining dispersed nuclear firms and industry institutes into a streamlined and efficient structure, a process that would take years. The foundation of the Corporation created new opportunities for the advancement of nuclear power and science, as well as a considerable expansion of the Corporation's international footprint. Today, ROSATOM is a multidimensional organization that is both one of Russia's largest and a global leader in nuclear technology, with a focus on research and development.

Chapter 1

History of the Soviet Union

spans the period from the establishment of Stalinism through victory in World War II and the death of Joseph Stalin in 1953, a period that comprises those years prior to and succeeding his death. In addition to assassinating his rivals, Stalin employed central planning to fundamentally transform Soviet society, particularly through the forced collectivization of agriculture and the rapid rise of heavy industry. Stalin solidified his hold on power throughout the party and the state while developing a strong personality cult around him.

The Soviet secret police and the Communist Party's mass mobilization were two of Stalin's most effective methods for infiltrating and influencing Soviet society. The tactics Stalin used to achieve his goals, which included party purges, political persecution of the general citizenry, and forced collectivization, including in Gulag labour camps and during famine, resulted in the deaths of millions of people, including children.

Soviet historians refer to World War II as "the Great Patriotic War" because it wrecked havoc on practically all of the Soviet Union, with approximately one out of every three World War II deaths being members of the Soviet Union. While fighting in World War II, the Soviet Union's armies occupied Eastern Europe, where they established or supported communist puppet states. There had been a war between the Western and Eastern (Soviet) Blocs by 1949. In Europe, the Warsaw Pact (formed in 1955) was pitted against NATO, which had been set up in 1949, by then. Stalin did not directly participate in any wars after 1945, instead opting to sustain his dictatorial rule until his death in 1953, when the Soviet Union collapsed.

The Soviet Union's development over time

State planning deployed resources to support the expansion of the country's manufacturing base. Between 1928 and 1932, the amount of pig iron produced increased from 3.3 million to 6.2 million tons per year, which was necessary for the expansion of the industrial infrastructure in the

United States. In the period from 35.4 million to 64 million tons, coal production climbed by a factor of two, while iron ore production increased by a factor of five, from 5.7 million to 19 million tons, both of which are crucial fuels for modern economies and Stalinist industrialization. A number of major projects, including the Magnitogorsk and Kuznetsk nuclear power plants, the Moscow and Gorky automobile plants, the Ural Mountains and Kramatorsk heavy machinery plants, and the Kharkiv, Stalingrad, and Chelyabinsk tractor plants, had been completed or were currently under construction.

Rather than improving, laborers' living standards tended to deteriorate as a result of industrialisation, rather than improving. As a result of Stalin's efforts to "tighten work discipline," the situation grew worse. For example, a 1932 amendment to the RSFSR labour law code allowed for the dismissal of employees who had been absent from work for one day without good reason.

The consequences of being fired included losing "the right to use ration and commodity cards," "the privilege to use an apartment," and the possibility of being blacklisted for future employment, all of which put you at risk of starving in the future. That said, those actions were not fully followed because managers were unable to replace the personnel who were affected. The 1938 legislation, on the other hand, was passed, bringing in labour books and making significant changes to the labour code. Managers who failed to put these laws into effect might risk criminal prosecution. In some cases, being absent or even 20 minutes late was sufficient grounds for dismissal.

Later that year, on June 26, 1940, the Supreme Soviet's Presidium published a decree "On the Implementation of the Eight-Hour Working Day, the Seven-Day Work Week, and the Prohibition of Unauthorized Departure by Labourers' and Office Workers from Factories and Offices", which replaced the 1938 modifications with mandatory criminal penalties for quitting a job (2–4 months jail), being late for work by 20 minutes (6 months probation and a 25% pay confiscation), and so

As a result of these figures, the Soviet authorities said that the Five-Year Industrial Production Plan had been completed by 93.7 percent in only four years, with heavy industry products accounting for 108 percent of total production. Stalin announced to the Central Committee in December 1932 that the plan had been a success, saying that increased coal and iron production would provide the necessary energy for future development.

Boosted by substantial investment made in the first five years after its implementation, industry flourished at a dizzying pace during the second five-year plan (1933–1937), coming close to meeting its targets and exceeding them. To put it another way, coal production had surged to 127 million tons by 1937, pig iron production had increased to 14.5 million tons, and the armaments industry had expanded at an alarming rate.

The First Five-Year Plan, while it significantly increased industrial capacity, was extremely taxing for industrial employees; quotas were difficult to reach, and miners were required to work 16 to 18-hour days on average.

If quotas are not fulfilled, treason charges may be brought against the company. [10] The working environment was poor, if not downright unsafe. A famine occurred as a result of the distribution of resources for the industry, as well as the decline in production that has occurred since collectivization of agriculture. During the development of industrial complexes, Gulag inmates were used as expendable resources, much like slave labor.

Things, on the other hand, quickly improved during the second plan. Throughout the 1930s, industrialization was associated with a rapid expansion in technical and engineering education, as well as an increasing emphasis on weapons production and development.

From 1921 through 1954, the police state was at its most aggressive, chasing down everyone who might be suspected of undermining the regime's authority. The figures that have been estimated have a wide range of values. The Chinese government sentenced approximately 3.7 million people for alleged counter-revolutionary offenses, with 600,000 being executed and 2.4 million being imprisoned in labour camps.

A further 700,000 were banished from the country. This period of Stalinist persecution culminated in the Great Purge of 1937–1938, which resulted in the expulsion of many experienced managers and experts as well as a major reduction in industrial production in 1937.

CHAPTER 2

THE ECONOMY

A group of farmers have come together to form a group.

Under the NEP, individual farmers would still be able to raise their own food, which Lenin had to accept as a given (New Economic Policy).

At least 20 years later, he decided to try and get it under the control of the state. In the meantime, he would work on economic growth. After Stalin came to power, the timetable for collectivization was slashed to just five years.

With the use of new, forceful methods, the demand for food rose, especially in the USSR's most important grain-producing areas. They had to give up their private land plots and other things when they joined kolkhozes (community farms). This is how it worked:

The state bought Kolkhoz food at a low price that the state set every harvest. In November 1929, the Central Committee's Plenum decided to force collectivization. The natural process of collectivization, on the other hand, was very slow. In any case, Russian peasant culture was a strong defense of tradition, which slowed down the Soviet state's plans.

In order to feed the growing number of people living in cities and make more money from wheat exports, the state wanted more control over agriculture. This was in line with the goals of the first Five Year Plan. Due to its late start, the USSR had to buy a lot of high-tech equipment for heavy industrialization.

Around 90% of Soviet agriculture was owned by the government by 1936. Peasants were sometimes angry at this process, so they killed their animals instead of giving them to collective farms.

Even though the government only wanted the grain, the peasants were still angry. People who were rich peasants were forced to move to Kazakhstan, Siberia, and parts of Russia's far north (a large portion of the kulaks served at forced labor camps). Then, anyone who didn't like collectivization was called a "kulak." In 1929, Stalin started to get rid of the kulaks as a group. Some people were killed, but a lot more people were sent to special settlements or forced labor camps.

Despite what people said, collectivization led to a huge drop in farm output, which would not return to pre-NEP levels until 1940. Collectivization caused a lot of trouble in Ukraine and the mostly Ukrainian Volga region. Instead of giving up their animals, peasants killed them in large groups.

25 percent of the country's cattle, sheep, and goats were slaughtered in a single year, and one-third of the country's pigs died as a result.

The Soviet number of cattle didn't get back to 1928 levels until the 1980s. Government administrators were sent to the countryside to "teach" peasants how to grow food in a socialist way, relying mostly on theories that had no basis in reality.

Even when the state was sure to win and collectivization was inevitable, the peasants tried to stop it. They farmed a lot less of their land and worked a lot less. Many Ukrainian academics think that the famine in Ukraine was caused by a plan to kill the Ukrainian people. Others say that the huge death toll was unavoidable because of a poorly planned attack on all peasants, who were mostly against Lenin and Stalin.

By the end of 1937, collective farms had taken over most of the land that was used for farming. In these years, up to 5 million people died as a result of persecution or starvation, but it isn't known for sure how many people died. Ukrainians and Kazakhs were hit more than most other countries were, though.

During the early Soviet era, a poster said: "The breath of Soviet Russia is the smoke from chimneys."

The number of people who died in the famines in Ukraine alone is now thought to be more than 3.5 million.

Estonia, Latvia, and Lithuania were taken over by the Soviet Union in 1940; the Germans took them over in 1941 and took them back in 1944. In 1948, their farms were owned together. All the peasants were intimidated, killed, and sent away by the government by 1952. All of the other Soviet republics saw a big drop in agricultural production.

INDUSTRIALIZATION IS SPEEDING UP.

Before World War II, during a time of rapid industrialization and huge collectivization, Soviet employment figures grew at a rate that was almost impossible to keep up. As of 1923, there were supposed to be 3.9 million jobs a year, but the number actually went up to 6.4 million. By 1937, the number had reached almost 7.9 million. It reached 8.3 million in 1940. Between 1926 and 1930, the number of people living in cities grew by 30 million people. Unemployment was a problem in late Imperial Russia and even during the NEP, but after Stalin's huge industrialization plan was put into place, it went away.

The rapid mobilization of resources needed to industrialize a society that had been mostly rural led to a severe labor shortage; unemployment was almost nonexistent. Soviet planners also played a role in the big drop in unemployment, which fell by half in real terms between 1928 and 1940. Having salaries artificially low, the government could hire far more people than would be possible in an open market. With the goal of getting raw materials for both military and consumer goods, a lot of big-scale extraction projects began.

Because so few individuals in the Soviet Union could afford to purchase a car, the Moscow and Gorky automobile manufacturers produced vehicles for the general population to purchase. Steel production and other industrial materials made it possible to make more cars. In 1931, for example, more than 200,000 cars and trucks were made.

CHAPTER 3

SOCIETY AND PROPAGANDA

Most leading communists in the 1920s and 1930s had previously worked as propagandists or editors before 1917, and they were well aware of the importance of propaganda at the time. When they came to power in 1917, there were a lot more publications, magazines, and pamphlets available.

They also took control of all communication media. In the 1930s, radio was a big thing.

People like Stalin worked as editors for the Pravda. There were a lot of local periodicals, as well as newspapers and magazines in all of the main languages, and the national newspapers "PRAVDA" and "Izvestia," which were both very popular. During the Soviet era, everyone agreed on everything. Until the 1980s, typewriters and printing presses were tightly controlled to make sure they didn't get used for illegal purposes.

The illegal distribution of revolutionary literature and nonfiction through Samizdat was a big deal. The few exceptions to the official media's homogeneity were a sign of high-level battle. Examples: The draft constitution from 1936 is a good one to look at.

Pravda and Trud both said that the draft constitution was good (the daily representing manual workers). When Izvestia was in charge, Nikolai Bukharin was in charge of it. He ran it, and it ran negative letters and reports about him. People in the party changed their line after Bukharin won the election. They began to attack "Trotskyite" opponents and traitors. As soon as 1937 came around and Bukharin was found and put on trial, he was hanged.

EDUCATION

A program was launched at the same time as industrialization to ensure that the number of schools and the overall quality of education both increased significantly in the following decades. Industrial workers needed to be educated to be able to compete. People went to 118,558 schools in 1927. 9.7 million people went to 166,275 schools in 1933.

Furthermore, by 1933, there were 900 specialized departments and 566 institutions that were already in place and working well. As a result, literacy rates went up a lot, especially in Central Asian countries.

WOMEN

It was also good for the people in the Soviet Union. Men and women were supposed to be able to get the same kind of education and work the same jobs. Even though these goals were not met in practice, the efforts to achieve them and the declaration of theoretical equality led to a general rise in the socioeconomic status of women. During the 1930s, women were hired as clerks for the growing number of department stores.

This led to a "feminization" of the industry as the percentage of female sales employees rose from 45 percent in 1935 to 62% in 1938. Propaganda started in 1931 tried to link femininity with "culture" and say that the New Soviet Woman was also a working woman.

This was partly due to the propaganda that was put forth. Many men didn't want to work as salespeople in the Soviet Union because they didn't like the job. Instead, poor-educated working-class women and women who had recently moved to the city from the countryside were hired as salespeople.

In addition, under Stalin's rule, the quality of medical care significantly improved, compared to Imperial times. Health care and education in the Soviet Union were made universally free thanks to Stalin's policies. People were vaccinated against diseases like typhus and cholera in the first generation, so they didn't have to worry about them. In the mid-to-late 1950s, these illnesses were uncommon, and infant mortality rates were at their lowest point in history during this time period.. Life expectancy for men and women increased by 20 years as a result. People in their 20s and 30s

Lenin was the driving force behind the creation of the Komsomol, or Young Communist League. Fast, it became an important tool in the spread of communism throughout the Soviet Union, and it was frequently called upon to fight against the Soviet Union's traditional foes as well.

It was through the Komsomol that the values of the Communist Party could be instilled in the next generation. In addition, the Komsomol was a place where labor and political activism could be quickly moved. They had the ability to relocate quickly to high-priority areas. In the 1920s, the Kremlin tasked the Komsomol with the primary responsibility of modernizing Soviet enterprises. In 1929, the

Stalingrad tractor plant employed 7,000 Komsomol cadets, the Ural factories employed 56,000, and the coal mines employed 36,000. It went like this: Bolshevik activists who were enthusiastic about communism's ideology were an important part of the plan. Because of this, they were able to influence their co-workers in the factories and mines, where this ideology was at its heart.

A meritocratic, supposedly class-neutral, membership policy was put in place by the Komsomol in 1935. As a result, fewer young people from the working class joined the military, while the number of people with higher levels of education increased. A new social structure was created as young professionals and students became part of the Soviet elite and proletariat were pushed out of the way.

The Komsomol's membership procedures demonstrate the extent to which Stalinism extended beyond the organization's walls. A combination of Leninist rhetoric and pragmatics was used to attract the most dedicated and skilled members.

MODERNITY

For the first time, women in Stalin's cities could give birth in a hospital with prenatal care, which coincided with the modernization of western countries. As the economy improved, so did the quality of education, just like in other developed countries.

At the time, the first group of people who were nearly all literate was formed. On a short-term basis, dozens of foreign engineers were hired to work in Russia. New industrial technology was learned by some engineers who were sent abroad.

Many new railways were constructed, but they were done so using slave labour, resulting in the deaths of many people along the route. Because they received extra help with their work, many of these employees were "set up" to do well, but they still received generous rewards for their efforts. Propaganda based on their achievements followed.

RELIGION

A long-term attack on the Russian Orthodox Church began as soon as the Bolsheviks took power in 1917. Stalin ramped up his an religious campaign in the 1930s. [30] In total, over a million pastors were imprisoned or killed, and the vast majority of religious institutions were closed. Orthodox clergymen were either killed or imprisoned in large numbers from 1918 to 1929, according to historian Dimitry Pospielovski. Between 1930 and 1939, another 45,000 people were slain or imprisoned. They also killed an additional 40,000 people who were employed by the monks and nuns.

Atheists were encouraged by the government, which claimed that religion was a byproduct of capitalism. In 1937, Pope Pius XI condemned Soviet religious intolerance.

In 1940, there were only a handful of churches still in operation. The Russian Orthodox Church was a powerful symbol of the czarist regime during the early years of Lenin's anti-religion campaign. In the 1930s, people of all religious backgrounds were targeted. Minority Christian organizations, Muslims, Jews, and Buddhists were all included in this grouping. Over time, atheism failed to convert many individuals to its way of life. It was during World War II when religion became more prominent in the shadows. To counter the Nazi threat, it was put to good use. It grew more popular in the 1990s. In Paul Froese's opinion,

It was a 70-year battle against religion fought by atheists in the Soviet Union When it came to promoting atheism, the Communist Party did the following: they demolished religious buildings, killed religious leaders, and pushed "scientific atheism," which included practices like atheist rites and the promise of temporal redemption. Prior Soviet citizens retained their religious convictions; but, a new generation of people who were too young to recall life under the USSR began to have religious convictions as well.

Only approximately 15 percent of Russians claim to not believe in God, while about 27 percent say they don't adhere to any particular religious faith.

CHAPTER 4

THERE HAS BEEN A START TO THE PURGE.

Stalin rose to near-absolute control by assassinating everybody who stood in his way. It is estimated that between 1936 and 1938, over 750,000 Soviets were slaughtered and more than a million were forced to work in labor camps for years. In the wake of Stalin's Great Terror, industry directors and engineers, as well as the majority of the Army's highest-ranking officers, were all but wiped out.

The assassination of Sergey Kirov in 1934 was the catalyst for this approach. As a result of which many believe Stalin was behind (despite there being no proof to support this). Those Bolsheviks who were alive in 1918 were largely expelled. In 1927, Trotsky was expelled from the Communist Party of the Soviet Union.

He was deported to Kazakhstan in 1928, afterwards banished from the Soviet Union in 1929, and eventually assassinated in 1940 in his homeland. Stalin utilized the purges to rid himself of political and physical enemies (as well as erstwhile pals) in high places. They were planning to overthrow Stalin, he claimed, citing Grigory Zinoviev and Lev Kamenev. As soon as the suspects were tortured and made to confess to being spies and saboteurs, they were convicted and executed.

Municipal courts across Russia were able to gain valuable lessons from Moscow's numerous sham trials. In December 1936, sixteen persons were put on trial.

The Seventeen were then put on trial in January 1937. Twenty-one were put to trial in June 1937. Many defendants in these cases admitted to acts like sabotage and spying, as well as counter-revolutionary plans and plans to invade and partition the Soviet Union with Germany and Japan. OGPU members led by Genrikh Yagoda carried out the first experiments in 1935 and 1936. The prosecution was then executed.

The "Bloody Dwarf," Nikolai Yezhov, was given command of the secret police.

When the "Great Purge" occurred in 1937, it wiped out the Soviet Union. During the reign of Yezhov, there was a time known as "Yezhovschina." It was well publicized. Incredibly high numbers of people were arrested. A total of 34,000 military members were let go, many of whom held important positions. A lot of members of the Politburo and Central Committee were thrown out, but the whole group was kept. Many academics, bureaucrats, and factory owners had also been evicted. During the Yezhovschina, two million people were imprisoned or executed.

 At the end of 1938, Stalin decided to put an end to the widespread purges because they were wreaking havoc on the country's infrastructure. Over time, Yezhov's influence waned. During the war, Yezhov lost all of his rights. He was tried and killed in 1940. Lavrentiy Beria, Stalin's buddy from Georgia, was named leader of the NKVD following his death (from 1938 to 1945). The Yezhovschina lasted until 1952, but nothing like it ever happened again.

A large number of people were imprisoned or murdered without trial during this time period for their perceived opposition to Stalin's leadership by the secret police. Between 1937 and 1938, the NKVD was responsible for the deaths of 681,692 persons, many of whom were political prisoners who were forced to work in the Gulag. The Soviet Union's widespread terror and purges were not well known outside the country. Some intellectuals and fellow travellers in the West believed that the

Soviets had developed a viable alternative to capitalist society in the Soviet Union. Freedom of expression, religion, and assembly were all spelled down in the country's first formal constitution, adopted in 1936.

In March of 1939, they met for the first time at the 18th party meeting in Moscow. The majority of 1934's 17th Congress attendees had already returned home. To defeat Nazi Germany, Litvinov lauded Stalin and chastised western democracies for failing to implement "collective security" principles..

INTERPRETING THE PURGES

Two major lines of interpretation have emerged among historians. One argues that the purges reflected Stalin's ambitions, his paranoia, and his inner drive to increase his power and eliminate potential rivals. Revisionist historians explain the purges by theorizing that rival factions exploited Stalin's paranoia and used terror to enhance their own position. Peter Whitewood examines the first purge, directed at the Army, and comes up with a third interpretation that: Stalin and other top leaders, assuming that they were always surrounded by enemies, always worried about the vulnerability and loyalty of the Red Army. It was not a ploy – Stalin truly believed it. "Stalin attacked the Red Army because he seriously misperceived a serious security threat"; thus "Stalin seems to have genuinely believed that foreign-backed enemies had infiltrated the ranks and managed to organize a conspiracy at the very heart of the Red Army." The purge hit deeply from June 1937 and November 1938, removing 35,000; many were executed. Experience in carrying out the purge facilitated purging other key elements in the wider Soviet polity.

Historians often cite the disruption as factors in its disastrous military performance during the German invasion.

1927–1939: FOREIGN RELATIONS

During the formation of the RSFSR and the USSR, the Soviet government forfeited foreign-owned commercial firms. There was no monetary or material remuneration for foreign investors. The USSR likewise refused to pay foreign debtors tsarist-era debts. Because of its openly proclaimed purpose of helping the overthrow of capitalist governments, the new Soviet republic was a pariah. It backed workers' uprisings in a number of capitalist European countries, but they all failed. With the NEC, Lenin reversed radical experiments and reintroduced a form of capitalism. The Comintern was told to stop planning uprisings. Lenin began seeking commerce, credit, and recognition in 1921. Foreign powers began to reopen trade lines and recognize the Soviet authority one by one.

In 1933, the United States was the last major power to recognize the Soviet Union. The French government suggested an alliance in 1934, and 30 countries agreed to ask the Soviet Union to join the League of Nations. The USSR had gained legitimacy, but in December 1939, it was ousted for aggression against Finland.

Stalin pushed for a socialist agenda in 1928, based on his assumption that capitalism was about to face a major catastrophe. Various European communist parties were told to avoid forming partnerships and to label moderate socialists as fascists instead. Activists were sent into labour unions to usurp leadership from socialists, an act that the British unions never forgot. By 1930, the Stalinists had begun to advocate for forming alliances with other political groups, and by 1934, the idea of forming a Popular Front had arisen. Willi Münzenberg, a Comintern operative, was particularly successful in enlisting intellectuals, antiwar, and pacifist groups to join the anti-Nazi coalition. To combat fascism, communists would create partnerships with any party. The Popular Front was merely an expedient for Stalinists, but it represented the ideal form of socialist transition for rightists.

Because the USSR officially opposed the 1919 World War I peace settlement, which France vehemently supported, Franco-Soviet relations were initially strained. While the Soviet Union wanted to acquire Eastern European lands, France was committed to safeguard the region's young republics.

Adolf Hitler's foreign policy, on the other hand, was oriented on a When Hitler withdrew from the Geneva World Disarmament Conference in 1933, the threat of a massive seizure of Central European, Eastern European, and Russian lands for Germany's own ends became real. The Soviet Foreign Minister, Maxim Litvinov, reversed Soviet policy on the Paris Peace Treaty, which led to

Franco-Soviet reconciliation. As early as May of 1935, the USSR and France and Czechoslovakia inked agreements on mutual defence and military aid. Stalin ordered the Comintern to join forces with leftist and centrist parties to form a popular front against Fascism. The agreement was harmed by strong ideological animosity toward the Soviet Union and the Comintern's new front in France, Poland's unwillingness to allow the Red Army on its country, France's defensive military posture, and the Soviet Union's continued involvement in repairing relations with Nazi Germany.

The Soviet Union assisted far-left militants in coming to Spain as volunteers and offered military aid, including weaponry and men, to the Republican faction in the Second Spanish Republic. The Spanish government gave the Soviet Union control of the country's treasury. Soviet troops often killed anarchist allies of the Spanish government. An anti-Bolshevik backlash against Moscow's assistance for the government in Paris and London made intervention in the war more difficult for Anglo-French allies to support.

The Anti-Comintern Pact was formed by Nazi Germany, Imperial Japan, Fascist Italy, and a number of Central and Eastern European countries (including Hungary), purportedly to restrict Communist activities but, more realistically, to build an alliance against the Soviet Union.

Stalin signed the Molotov–Ribbentrop Pact, a non-aggression pact with Nazi Germany, and the German–Soviet Commercial Agreement, which established commercial cooperation, on August. In a secret appendix to the treaty, Eastern Poland, Latvia, Estonia, Bessarabia, and Finland were granted to the USSR, while Nazi Germany obtained Western Poland and Lithuania. This reflected the Soviet Union's intention to expand its borders.

After striking a contract with Hitler in 1939–1940, Stalin conquered half of Poland, the three Baltic States, and Romania's Northern Bukovina and Bessarabia. They were no longer buffers between the Soviet Union and German regions, according to Louis Fischer. Hitler was supported by them as he marched towards Moscow's gates.

Propaganda improved foreign relations as well. To establish international influence and persuade fellow travellers and pacifists to create popular fronts, international exhibitions, the distribution of media such as Alexander Nevski's films, and the invitation of notable foreign persons to tour the Soviet Union were used.

CHAPTER 5
THE SECOND WORLD WAR BEGINS [EDITED]

Poland was occupied by Germany and the Soviet Union on September 1, and the two countries were at war until September 17. To crush opposition, the Soviets executed and jailed tens of thousands of people. From 1939 through 1941, they deported suspected ethnic groups to Siberia in four waves. Estimates range from around 1.5 million to over 2 million people.

Stalin put territorial demands on Finland in exchange for points that would safeguard Leningrad if Poland were partitioned between Germany and the Soviet Union. Stalin invaded as a result of Helsinki's reluctance, which was backed by international opinion.

Despite outnumbering Finnish forces by more than 2.5 to 1, the Red Army found the fight to be embarrassingly tough due to a lack of winter equipment and competent leadership following the purge of the Soviet high command. The Finns fought back valiantly, and the Allies encouraged and sympathized with them. In March 1940, Finland proposed an armistice in response to a new threat. It was obliged to relinquish the Karelian Isthmus and other minor territories.

As a result, the Soviet army's poor performance was perceived by London, Washington, and especially Berlin as evidence that the Soviet army was incapable of defending the Soviet Union against an invasion by the Nazis.

In 1940, the Soviet Union unlawfully conquered and annexed Lithuania, Latvia, and Estonia. The Soviet Union carried out the first significant deportations from Lithuania, Latvia, and Estonia on June 14, 1941.

On June 26, 1940, the Soviet government issued an ultimatum to Romania's minister in Moscow, demanding that Romania promptly deliver over Bessarabia and Northern Bukovina. Italy and Germany pressured King Carol II to do so because they needed Romania's stability and access to its oil reserves. Carol agreed under duress because she had no hope of receiving assistance from France or the United Kingdom. Bessarabia, Northern Bukovina, and Hertsa were taken on June 28 when Soviet soldiers crossed the Dniester River.

SOVIET KIDS CELEBRATE THE END OF THE SCHOOL YEAR ON THE EVE OF THE GREAT PATRIOTIC WAR, JUNE 21, 1941.

On June 22, 1941, Adolf Hitler attacked the Soviet Union, blatantly violating the covenant of non-aggression. Nothing had been planned by Stalin. After German disinformation confused Soviet intelligence, the assault caught the Soviet forces off guard. Invasion was predicted by Stalin in the long term, but not so swiftly.

The Purges had completely devastated the Army, and it would take a long time for it to recover. As a result, there was no mobilization, and the Soviet Army arrived at the assault unprepared operationally. In the opening weeks of the fight, hundreds of thousands of troops were killed, maimed, or abducted, making it a disaster. Entire divisions crumbled in the face of the German assault. Because of poor treatment, just one-tenth of Red Army POWs survived German prison camps. In comparison, just roughly a third of German POWs survived their captivity in Soviet prison camps. German troops reached the outskirts of Moscow in December 1941 but were unable to conquer it due to persistent Soviet defence and counterattacks. During the Battle of Stalingrad in 1942–1943, the Red Army annihilated the German army. Because the Japanese were hesitant to open a second front in Manchuria, the Soviets were able to bring dozens of Red Army divisions back from eastern Russia.

These forces were crucial in changing the tide because most of their officer corps had escaped Stalin's purges. Over the entire German front line, Soviet forces launched massive counter-offensives. By 1944, the Germans had been forced out of the Soviet Union and into the Vistula River valley, just east of Prussia. The arrival of Soviet Marshal Georgy Zhukov from Prussia and Marshal Ivan Konev from the south, who divided Germany in half, cemented Nazi Germany's doom. On May 2, 1945, the last German troops surrendered in Berlin to ecstatic Soviet troops.

CHANGES IN THE WAR

Large sections of eastern Germany were occupied by the Soviet Union from the end of 1944 to 1949, and the capital city of Berlin was taken on 2 May 1945, while over fifteen million Germans were displaced from eastern Germany and pushed into central and western Germany (later known as the German Democratic Republic) (later called the Federal Republic of Germany).

During the war, the Soviet Union was engulfed in a patriotic emergency, and the persecution of the Orthodox Church came to an end. The Church was now given some leeway as long as it stayed out of politics. An updated version of the Soviet national anthem, the Internationale, was created in 1944 to replace the original, which had been in use since 1918. People were deemed to respond better to a fight for their nation than a political doctrine, therefore these alterations were made.

Because the West didn't create a second land front in Europe until the invasion of Italy and the Battle of Normandy, the Soviet Union suffered the brunt of World War II. It is estimated that over 26.6 million Soviets died throughout the war, with 18 million of them being civilians. In many of the Nazi-conquered cities, civilians were picked up and burned or shot. [Required citation] The retreating Soviet army was commanded to follow a "scorched earth" policy, in which withdrawing Soviet troops were told to destroy civilian infrastructure and food supplies so that Nazi German soldiers would not have been able to exploit them.

Nikita Khrushchev updated Stalin's original declaration of 7 million combat deaths in March 1946 to a round figure of 20 million in 1956. Demographers at the State Statistics Committee (Goskomstat) re-evaluated the population in the late 1980s and estimated it to be between 26 and 27 million people. There have been a number of additional estimations offered.

Two-thirds of the estimated deaths were civilians, according to the most detailed estimates. The distribution of war casualties by nationality, on the other hand, is less widely understood. While major Slavic groups suffered the greatest aggregate human losses, minority nationalities, primarily from European Russia, suffered the greatest losses relative to population size, according to one study based on indirect evidence from the 1959 population census. Minority nationalities were among the groups whose men were mustered to the front in "nationality battalions" and appear to have suffered disproportionately.

Conquering and occupying Eastern Europe after World War II was in conformity with Soviet doctrine.

Stalin was very strict about punishing people who he thought were working with Germany during the war, as well as dealing with the issue of nationalism, which he thought was a threat to the Soviet Union's unity. There were a lot of people from different ethnic groups who were sent to Siberian gulags.

Some of these people were reservists who were executed in the spring of 1940, after the Nazis took eastern Poland in 1939. This was known as the Katyn massacre. Another group of people was sent to Siberia and Central Asia in the years 1941, 1943, and 1944: the Volga Germans, Chechen, and Ingush people. They were also sent to Kazakhstan and Central Asia. Even though these groups were officially "rehabilitated," some of the areas they used to have control over were never given back to them.

Stalin also said that the Russian people helped defeat the Nazis in a famous Victory Day toast in May 1945: "In honor of the health of our Soviet people and, above all, of the Russian people, I would like to raise a glass. First of all, I raise a glass to the health of the Russian people, because they were widely known as the main force of the Soviet Union in this war. And the Russian people's faith in the Soviet government was the most important thing that led to the historic victory over fascism that changed the world."

World War II wreaked havoc across Eurasia, from the Atlantic to the Pacific oceans. Almost no country was left untouched. For decades, the Soviet Union built up a strong base in manufacturing. Then in the 1930s, a lot of that foundation went away. In 1946–1948, the Soviet Union went through a famine caused by war damage that killed an estimated 1 to 1.5 million people, as well as a secondary population loss because of less fertility. [a] As time went on and more people died in World War II, the Soviet Union regained its production capacity and even surpassed it. It became the country with the most powerful land army in history and the most powerful military production capabilities.

THERE WAS A LOT OF INDUSTRIAL AND MILITARY GROWTH UNDER STALIN.

Despite getting help and weapons from the US under the Lend-Lease program, the Soviet Union made more war materials than Nazi Germany because of the rapid growth of Soviet industrial production during the interwar years. The extra supplies from lend-lease made up about 10% to 13% of the Soviet Union's own industrial output. 18 million tons of steel and 128 million tons of coal were made under the Second Five-Year Plan. Steel and coal were made before the Third Five Year Plan was stopped.

The Soviet Union had a lot of industrial output, which led to an armaments industry that helped the army fight back against the Nazis. This quote from Robert L. Hutchings says that if there had been a slower rise in industry, the attack would have been successful and world history would have been very different. [68] Factory workers, on the other hand, had a hard time of it, too. Workers were urged to fulfill and surpass quotas through propaganda campaigns, such as those promoted by the Stakhanovism movement.

There are some people who believe that the Soviet Union's lack of ability to defend itself was a flaw in Stalin's economic plan, on the other hand. David Shearer, for example, says that there was a "command-administrative economy," but it wasn't "planned" to be there. Claims: He says that the Soviet Union was still reeling from the Great Purge, and was completely unprepared for the Germans to come in and attack. economist Holland Hunter also says that there were a lot of "alternative paths" that could have led to the same good results as those achieved by 1936, but with far less turbulence, waste, destruction, and sacrifice. This is from his book, The Overambitious First Soviet Five-Year Plan.

COLD WAR

Before and after World War II, the Soviet Union expanded its political and military control over parts of Europe that were part of the Russian Empire. Some saw this as a continuation of what the Russian Empire did. Following World War II, the

Soviet Union took over the Baltic States and the eastern parts of interwar Poland. They had been lost by the Soviet Union in the Treaty of Brest-Litovsk (1918).

That's not all. The German government also gave Russia the northern half of East Prussia (Kaliningrad Oblast). Ukrainian SSR bought Zakarpattia Oblast from Czechoslovakia and Chernivtsi Oblast from Romania, which were both in Czechoslovakia. Elections were held in Poland, Czechoslovakia, Hungary, Romania, and Bulgaria in the late 1940s, and pro-Soviet Communist Parties won. Peoples political Democratic governments were established in these regions of the world by the end of the century. These elections are widely thought to be manipulated, and Western countries have called them "show elections." During the Cold War, the countries of Eastern Europe became "satellites" of the Soviet Union. They were "independent" countries that were one-party communist states, but their General Secretary had to be approved by the Kremlin. Their governments tended to follow the Soviet Union's wishes, but nationalist forces and pressures in the satellite states played a role in deviating from strict Soviet rule.

CHAPTER 6

HOW THE SOVIET UNION AND THE UNITED STATES ARE GETTING ALONG THESE DAYS

Weapons, food, and gasoline were sent to the USSR by the US and the UK, mostly through Lend Lease. With Stalin striving to keep internal events shrouded under a veil of secrecy, the three powers kept constant communication with one another. Churchill and other senior Soviet officials, as well as Roosevelt's top aide Harry Hopkins, went to Moscow to see what was going on there. Stalin told the US and Britain to start a second front on the European continent many times.

 The Allied invasion did not happen until June 1944, nearly two years later. Meanwhile, the Russians lost a lot of people, and the Soviets took the brunt of the power of the German army. The Allies said that

Stalin didn't pay attention to the fact that the Allies used a lot of air power.

There was very strict censorship of both art and science, but it didn't stop them from being made. The Russian Association of Proletarian Writers (RAPP) said that politics was important in literary production, and it published content that mostly spoke about working-class values in fiction, where the All-Russian Union of Writers (AUW) had tried to publish apolitical writing.

Evgeny Zamyatin was the chairman of the AUW in 1925 when the RAPP began a campaign against hlm. A group called the All-Russian Union of Soviet Writers, which was very strict about writing in the socialist realism style, replaced the AUW. When Trofim Lysenko, a now-discredited Soviet biologist, said that Mendelian heredity was wrong, he had a big impact on Soviet biology. He said that a kind of Lamarckism was better.

The theory of relativity was thought of as "bourgeois idealism" in physics at the time. It was mostly done by Andrei Zhdanov, Stalin's "ideological hatchet man," until he died in 1948 of a heart attack at the age of 69. A portrait of Joseph Stalin was on display in every school, factory, and government office after the war. Even though he rarely spoke in public,

Stalin's cult of personality reached its peak in the postwar years. After the war, the focus was on heavy industries and energy, which meant that living standards didn't improve much outside of the big cities.

During the war, the Soviet Union made some small changes to its political system. These changes came to an end in 1945. Following the war, the Orthodox Church was mostly unaffected and was even allowed to print a small amount of religious literature. The persecution of other religions began again. A citation is needed. Generals such as Zhukov were demoted to regional commands when Stalin and the Communist Party were awarded full credit for the victory over Germany in the Second World War (Ukraine in his case). In response to the start of the Cold War, anti-Western propaganda became more aggressive, portraying the capitalist world as a rotten place full of crime and unemployment.

A "big deal" came to be between the Soviet nomenclature and experts, who had the same social status as the middle class in the West. The state would allow "bourgeois" habits like buying things, having sex, and having a home in exchange for their unwavering loyalty to the state.

The informal "big deal" came about as a result of World War II, when many middle-class people in the Soviet Union thought they would get a better standard of living after the war in exchange for their sacrifices. Because the Soviet system couldn't work without technical experts and nomenclature, the state needed their help.

The state's control was also loosened at some point during the conflict, which allowed for informal procedures that usually broke the rules to be used. After 1945, the state didn't completely get rid of social control. Instead, the state worked to get people to like them, allowing some rules to be broken as long as people stayed loyal to the government as a whole. There was a rise in materialism, corruption, and nepotism after the "great deal." This lasted for the rest of the Soviet Union's life. It was a big deal when a series of romance novels for women came out in the late 1940s. Before the war, this kind of book would have been unthinkable.

Vladimir Putin's "thieves in law," as organized crime in Russia is called, grew a lot in the late 1940s. This led to a new subculture with its own language and culture. In spite of their name, the vory in the law are not just thieves. They carry out a wide range of illegal activities. In a society where important goods were hard to come by, the vory v zakone did well as blackmarketeers. The crime wave that hit the Soviet Union in the late 1940s caused a lot of people to worry.

The rise in juvenile crime was a cause for concern. A police survey from 1947 found that youths under the age of 16 were responsible for 69% of all crimes. War orphans who were living on the streets turned to crime as a way to make money and live. Most of the accusations about juvenile crime were about street kids who were prostitutes, thieves, or hired to work for the vory v zakone.

As time went on, the Great Patriotic War came to be seen as a time of adventure, danger, and national solidarity, while life in the post-war era was seen as dull, boring, and uninteresting, and as a time when people put their own personal interests above the greater good.

The general belief was that even though the war had been won, the peace had been lost, because wartime dreams and hopes for a better world after the war had been crushed by the war itself.

During the postwar era, there were many different subcultures. Most of them were different from what the government approved in some way, like listening to smuggled records of Western pop music. The government either let them or tried to stop them, depending on the nature of the subcultures.

After World War II, another post-war social trend was individualism and a desire for solitude. People wanted to spend more time outside of cities in the countryside where the state had less control over how people lived. In the countryside, the nomenclature and their families could enjoy themselves without being seen by anyone else. This became the most important symbol for the nomenclature. Other people tried to get their own space by pursuing non-political interests like the hard sciences or moving to a place like Siberia, where the state had less power.

Svoi, informal networks of friends and relatives that worked as self-help groups, started to play a bigger role in determining one's social success. Being a member of the right svoi could help one's kids get into a good university or get basic goods like toilet paper. A further evidence of the social trend toward more personal spaces for regular people was the rise in popularity of underground poetry and samizdat literature that called into question the Soviet authorities.

Young people in the late 1940s preferred to hear the Voice of America and British Broadcasting Corporation (BBC) Russian language transmissions, even though the government tried to stop them. This led to a big campaign in 1948 to discredit both radio stations as "capitalist propaganda."

In the late 1940s, the magazines America (America) and Britanskii Soiuznik (British Ally) were hugely popular with young people, and they sold out in minutes when they arrived at kiosks in Moscow and Leningrad (modern St. Petersburg). In Juliane Fürst's opinion, young people's interest in English and American culture is not a rejection of the Soviet system, but rather a simple curiosity about the world outside of the Soviet Union.

 Many young people in the late 1940s and early 1950s, according to Fürst, had mixed feelings about their country. On the one hand, they thought their country was the best and most progressive in the world, but they also thought there might be something better out there.

The authorities were able to make people who didn't like the Soviet system seem "unpatriotic" because of the way Russian nationalism and Communism came together during the Great Patriotic War to form a new Soviet identity that was both proud to be Russian and proud to be a Communist. This seemed to fend off the parts of some people's self-doubt that were there at the time.

After 1945, the popularity of apolitical films like musicals, comedies, and romances over more political films that celebrated Communism was another sign that people were becoming more interested in having their own space.

In the late 1940s, the Soviet film industry couldn't keep up with demand because of postwar reconstruction problems. As a result, Soviet cinemas showed American and German films that the Red Army had taken from eastern Germany and Eastern Europe, which were called "trophy films" in the Soviet Union.

A lot of Soviet people liked American movies like Stagecoach, The Roaring Twenties, The Count of Monte Cristo (and Sun Valley), which made the government very unhappy. A German-Hungarian movie called "The Girl of My Dreams," which was released in 1947, and a movie called "Tarzan's New York Adventures," which was released in 1951. [84] In Tbilisi, the movie "The Girl of My Dreams," which had "amazing and incomprehensible" Marika Rökk in the lead role, was the only thing that everyone in the city went crazy for. In the metropolis, normal life came to a halt. All of a sudden, everyone was talking about the movie. They were going to see it as soon as they could. People were whistling songs from the movie in the street, and you could hear people playing the piano from half-open windows.

As early as the late 940s, the Austrian scholar Franz Burkina claimed that the Soviet government was not a monolithic totalitarian machine, but rather was divided into vast chefstvo (patronage) networks that extended down from the elite to the lowest levels of power, with Stalin serving as the ultimate arbiter of the various factions rather than the leader of a state in the manner of 1984.

As part of his research, Borkenau examined official Soviet pronouncements and the relative placement of various officials at the Kremlin on festive occasions in order to determine which Soviet representative seemed to have Stalin's authorization but which did not. Borkenau's methods included an in-depth examination of official Soviet pronouncements as well as the relative placement of various officials at the Kremlin on festive occasions to determine who had Stalin's approval and who did not. Journalistic editorials, formal guest lists, obituaries in Soviet newspapers, and transcripts of formal speeches were all useful in identifying the various chefstvo networks.

Borkenau argued that even minor shifts in the formalistic language of the Soviet state could signal significant shifts: "Political issues must be interpreted in the light of formulas, political and otherwise, and their history; and such interpretation cannot be safely concluded until the entire history of the given formula has been established from its first enunciation on."

Throughout the post-war period, the secret police frightened the general public. Despite the fact that nothing quite similar to the events of 1937 occurred again, there were numerous minor purges, including a massive purge of Georgia's political machinery in 1951–1952. In the United States, the greatest opposition to the state has been characterized as "rootless cosmopolitans," a term that has never been defined precisely. It was common practice to refer to intellectuals, Jews, and occasionally both, as "rootless cosmopolitans." Also following WWII, Stalin's health deteriorated precipitously. His stroke occurred in the fall of 1945, and he was confined to a hospital for a number of months. It was then that he suffered a second stroke in 1947. Instead of having party meetings, Stalin preferred to invite Politburo members to all-night dinners where he would compel them to become drunk and humiliate themselves or say something incriminating, rather than participating in day-to-day state administration.]

In October 1952, the Soviet Union hosted the first postwar party congress. Nikita Khrushchev and Georgy Malenkov made the crucial speeches while Stalin sat in quiet for the majority of the proceedings since he was not feeling well. The party should be renamed, though, as he suggested. "The All-Union Party of Bolsheviks was renamed "The Communist Party of the Soviet Union" on the grounds that "there was a time when it was vital to distinguish ourselves from the Mensheviks, but there are no Mensheviks any longer." We've completely taken over the party." Stalin also made a passing reference to his advancing age (he will turn 73 in two months) and intimated that it could be time for him to step down from his position. No one in the congress dared to oppose it, so the delegates instead pleaded with him to continue serving.

During a routine inspection of his Volynskoe dacha on March 1, 1953, Stalin's servants discovered him semi-conscious on the floor of his bedroom.

According to his doctor, he had had a cerebral haemorrhage.

A memorial service was held for Stalin on March 5, 1953. The cause of his death was determined to be a brain haemorrhage along with significant atherosclerosis-related damage to his cerebral arteries, according to the results of an autopsy performed in 1989. Assassination attempts on Stalin were possible. Beria has been suspected of murder, despite the fact that no tangible evidence has yet been presented against the accusation.

A succession plan or a system within which power might be transmitted were not left behind by Stalin.

A meeting of the Communist Party's Central Committee was held on the day of his death, with Malenkov, Beria, and Khrushchev emerging as the party's senior figures.

It was decided to reintroduce the system of collaborative leadership, with protections in place to prevent any one member from assuming autocratic power.

In accordance with the order of precedence presented formally on 5 March 1953, the collective leadership consisted of Georgy Malenkov, Lavrentiy Beria, Vyacheslav Molotov, Kliment Voroshilov, Nikita Khrushchev, Nikolai Bulganin, Lazar Kaganovich, and Anastasia Mikoyan, all members of the Presidium of the Central Committee of the Communist Party of the Soviet Union.

A number of changes were made to the Soviet system right away

The economic reforms limited large-scale construction projects, switched the emphasis to home construction, and reduced peasant taxes in order to increase output.

It was the new authorities' goal to bring the Korean War to a negotiated conclusion in July 1953, which they did by advocating rapprochement with Yugoslavia as well as a less confrontational relationship with the United States.

The doctors who had been detained were released, and the anti-Semitic purges were brought to an end.

"A huge amnesty was provided for persons imprisoned for non-political offenses, resulting in a 50% reduction in the country's jail population. The state security and Gulag systems were reorganized, and torture was abolished in April 1953."

CHAPTER 7

The Soviet Union was an Eastern European country.

Weapons of mass destruction

In the decade running up to World War II, Soviet physicists were significantly involved in nuclear and atomic research. As early as 1939, they had proved that when uranium is fashioned, each nucleus produces neutrons, which theoretically allows a chain reaction to begin. In the following year, physicists concluded that such a chain reaction could be initiated in either natural uranium or its isotope uranium-235, and that it could be sustained and controlled with the use of a moderator such as heavy water When the Soviet Academy of Sciences created the Uranium Commission in July 1940, it was to look into the "uranium problem."

By February 1939, Soviet physicists had learned of the discovery of nuclear fission in the West. Even if the military implications of such a discovery were evident at the time, the German invasion of the Soviet Union in June 1941 put a stop to Soviet investigation. Georgy N. Flerov, a Soviet physicist who worked in the United States during World War II, noticed that studies on nuclear fission were no longer appearing in Western magazines, indicating that nuclear fission research had been classified. Flurov responded by writing to Premier Joseph Stalin and others, emphasizing the importance of "immediately constructing a nuclear weapon from nuclear fuel."

When Stalin sanctioned the launch of a research project in 1943, it would be directed by Igor V. Kurchatov, the director of the nuclear physics laboratory of the Physico-Technical Institute of the Academy of Sciences in Leningrad at the time, who would be overseen by Igor V. Kurchatov and his team. To carry out the new plan, Laboratory No. 2 was established in April under the direction of Kurchatov.

In the aftermath of World War II, it was renamed the Russian Research Centre Kurchatov Institute, and eventually became the Laboratory of Measurement Devices of the Russian Academy of Sciences. As a result of receiving Western intelligence about the feasibility of plutonium as a weapon material, Kurchatov began working on three projects: designing an experimental uranium pile and achieving a chain reaction, exploring methods to separate the isotope uranium-235, and researching the properties of plutonium and how it might be produced.

Over the course of 1944, the scope of the initiative remained limited. Despite the fact that the war continued, the possibility of a genuine weapon loomed ominously in the horizon, and money was scarce, Kurchatov was able to keep the number of personnel employed by him to a minimal. By the time of the Potsdam Conference, which brought the leaders of the Allied nations together the day after the United States conducted the Trinity test in July 1945, the nuclear-weapons effort was poised to undergo a fundamental transition. The United States had discovered a "new weapon of amazing destructive force," according to Truman, during one of the conference's sessions. The Soviet leader expressed hope that the United States would "make effective use of it against the Japanese."

Upon learning of the United States' decision to drop two atomic bombs on Japan in early August 1945, Stalin grasped the significance of this new weapon and ordered a fast development push to produce an atomic bomb. The Soviet version of the Manhattan Project was controlled by a Special Committee directed by Lavrenty P. Beria, the commander of the NKVD, who served as the committee's chairman (Soviet secret police and ancestor of the KGB). It took four years for the Soviet Union to complete the weapon's development, which included extensive use of Gulag labour to mine uranium and build the weapon's manufacturing facilities.

A chain reaction involving an experimental graphite-moderated natural uranium pile known as F-1 took place on December 25, 1946, outside Moscow, marking the beginning of the Soviet nuclear age. On June 19, 1948, the Chelyabinsk-40 (later known as Chelyabinsk-65 and currently known as Ozersk) complex in the Ural Mountains became operational with the first plutonium production reactor, which was built by the Soviet Union.

The first batch of plutonium was generated eight months after the first batch of nuclear fuel. After being separated at a local radio-chemical facility, the irradiated uranium fuel was converted into plutonium metal and shaped into hemispheres in a nuclear reactor nearby. It was in the "Installation"

(KB-11), which was located in what would later become the secret Soviet city of Sarov, 400 kilometers (250 miles) southeast of Moscow, that the final assembly took place. Similarly to Los Alamos, the secret laboratory known as Arzamas-16 (now known as the All-Russian Scientific Research Institute of Experimental Physics) was where the world's first nuclear weapons were developed and built.

In 1950, after the arrests of the German-born Klaus Fuchs in the United Kingdom, and of the American couple Julius and Ethel Rosenberg in the United States, it became clear that espionage played an important role in the creation of the Soviet atomic weapon. Immediately after the Soviet Union's breakup in 1991, new information collected from Russian sources revealed that espionage was more pervasive than previously imagined and played a greater role in the Soviets' success than previously thought.

 Throughout the war and beyond, Beria's spies amassed vast amounts of technical data, allowing Kurchatov and his crew to save significant amounts of time and resources. It was on August 29, 1949, that the Soviet Union carried out its first nuclear test, employing a plutonium device (named Joe-1 in the West) with a yield of approximately 20 kilotons and a yield of roughly 20 kilotons. Joe-1 was based on designs provided by Fuchs and Theodore A. Hall, the latter of whom was a second significant spy at Los Alamos whose activities were only uncovered after the Soviet Union was dismantled. Fuchs and Hall were both killed in the fall of the Soviet Union. In fact, it was an exact replica of the Fat Man bomb, which was tested at Trinity and dropped on Nagasaki in 1945.

WEAPONS BASED ON THERMONUCLEAR FUSION ARE BEING DEVELOPED.

It was in June 1948 that Igor Y. Tamm was appointed to the position of director of a special research group at the P.N. Lebedev Physics Institute (FIAN) to investigate the feasibility of constructing a thermonuclear bomb. After joining Tamm's group, Andrey Sakharov worked on estimates provided by Yakov Zeldovich's group at the Institute of Chemical Physics, alongside his colleagues Vitaly Ginzburg and Yury Romanov, as well as on his own research. According to Sakharov, the Russian discovery of the fundamental concepts underlying the thermonuclear bomb progressed through a number of stages.

Sakharov first proposed the first concept in 1948, which consisted of alternating layers of deuterium and uranium-238 between a fissile core and a chemical high explosive encircling it. The concept was later refined and refined again. Using lithium-6 deuteride instead of liquid deuterium, Ginzburg came up with the Sloika concept in 1949, which was named after Ginzburg ("Layer Cake"). Upon being bombarded with neutrons, lithium-6 creates tritium, which can then be fused with deuterium to release even more energy. Lithium-6 is a radioactive element.

March 1950 marked the month that Sakharov arrived at KB-11. Work on developing and manufacturing Soviet nuclear weapons had begun at the KB-11 facility three years earlier, under the scientific direction of Yuly Khariton, who was now retired. Additionally, members of the Tamm and Zeldovich groups worked on KB-11 to develop a thermonuclear weapon. In the early hours of August

12, 1953, a 400-kiloton Layer Cake bomb, known in the West as Joe-4 and in the Soviet Union as RDS-6, went off in the United States. It was also the first time that solid lithium-6 deuteride was used, as well as the first time that a deliverable thermonuclear weapon was used, a milestone that the America still wouldn't reach till May 20, 1956. A more efficient two-stage nuclear arrangement utilizing radiation compression (similar to the Teller-Ulam concept) was finally tested and successfully exploded on November 22, 1955. An aircraft carried the thermonuclear bomb, which was known in the West as Joe-19 and in the Soviet Union as RDS-37, and dropped it from the sky above the Semipalatinsk (now Semey) test site in Kazakhstan. According to Sakharov, this test "crowned years of effort [and] prepared the way for a broad spectrum of devices with astounding capabilities...it had almost overcome the difficulty of developing high-performance thermonuclear weapons."

A total of 715 tests were carried out by the Soviet Union between 1949 and 1990, providing a diverse variety of weapons, ranging from nuclear artillery shells to multimegaton missile warheads and nuclear bombs. On October 30, 1961, the Soviet Union detonated a 58-megaton nuclear weapon, which was later determined to have been tested at a yield that was approximately half that of its optimal design yield.

CHAPTER 8

FRANCE

Among those who made significant contributions to atomic physics during the twentieth century were Henri Becquerel, Marie and Pierre Curie, and Frédéric and Irène Joliot-Curie, to name a few. Over the course of World War II, several French scientists collaborated on an Anglo-Canadian project in Canada that resulted in the development of a heavy water reactor in the town of Chalk River, Ontario, in 1945.

France's Atomic Energy Commission (Commissariat à l'Énergie Atomique; CEA) was established on October 18, 1945, by General Charles de Gaulle, with the intention of harnessing the potential of atomic energy for scientific, economic, and military purposes. Atomic energy was employed for the first time in a military application in 1951. In July 1952, the National Assembly passed a five-year plan, with the primary goal of constructing plutonium-producing reactors as its primary objective. The construction of a reactor at Marcoule began in the summer of 1954, followed by the establishment of a plutonium separation plant the following year.

On December 26, 1954, the French government debated whether or not to proceed with the development of an atomic weapon. Because of this, Prime Minister Pierre Mendès-France launched a clandestine nuclear-weapons production operation in order to build an atomic bomb. On November 30, 1956, a protocol was agreed upon establishing the responsibilities of the CEA and the Defense Ministry.

Plumptonium was provided, a gadget was manufactured, and a testing site was set up for the experiment. In the development of the atomic bomb, Pierre Guillaumat, Gen. Charles Ailleret, and Yves Rocard played pivotal roles, among others. On July 22, 1958, De Gaulle, now President of the United States, established the date for the first atomic detonation in the first three months of 1960, which occurred in the first three months of 1960.

For De Gaulle in particular, the accomplishment of the bomb by France signified the country's independence as well as the country's participation in global affairs. In 1960, France detonated an atomic bomb in the Sahara Desert, in what was then French Algeria, from an observation tower that measured 105 meters (344 feet). The plutonium implosion design yielded 60 to 70 kilotons of plutonium, which was three times the amount of plutonium created by the atomic bomb that was dropped on Nagasaki, Japan.

The French conducted three additional atmospheric tests in Algeria as well as 13 additional underground tests over the next six years, before relocating its test site to the Pacific Ocean's uninhabited atolls of Mururoa and Fangataufa, where it remains today. From 1966 until 1996, France carried out 194 nuclear tests in the Pacific Ocean. The outcome has been the development of ever-improving fission, boosted-fission, and two-stage thermonuclear weapons for use in a variety of weapon systems, including aircraft bombs and missiles, as well as ground and sea-based ballistic missiles.

Physicist Pierre Billaud's account of the French thermonuclear bomb development, published in 1997, provides information about the scientists who were involved in the discovery of basic principles. A key role in France's development of the thermonuclear weapon during this time, Billaud served as the director of the Centre de Limeil,

France's most important warhead design laboratory outside Paris, from 1966 to 1968.

Directed by Billaud, the CEA's division in charge of French nuclear warhead development and production following a successful test in February 1960, the Direction des Applications Militaires focused on modifying warheads for delivery by Mirage IV aircraft and refining fission weapon designs.

Afraid that China would reach the thermonuclear threshold before France, De Gaulle pushed hard for the CEA to come up with an answer, giving them until 1968 to do so. The CEA complex's Limeil facility and others were expanded in response to research into the fundamental concepts of matter and energy. The fundamental concept of radiation implosion was first proposed by physicist Michel Carayol in a publication from April 1967. There were no guarantees that this was the answer, and the search for a more definitive answer persisted.

William Cook, who oversaw the British thermonuclear program in the mid-1950s, endorsed Carayol's ideas. It wasn't the first time Cook had expressed skepticism about Carayol's ideas. The French embassy's military attaché in London was able to act fast because of Cook's verbal transmission of important intelligence. Most likely, the British government released this information for political reasons. De Gaulle's decision to block the United Kingdom from joining the Common Market was opposed by British Prime Minister Harold Wilson (European Economic Community). By sharing thermonuclear research with France, Wilson apparently thought that de Gaulle would give up his veto on nuclear weapons. This deception backfired as France refused to allow the British back into the nation on November 27, 1967.

After getting confirmation that Carayol's design was on the right track, France moved fast to put it to the test in its Pacific test site. It was August 24, 1968, when France became the first country to conduct a thermonuclear test, with an explosion of 2.6 megatons. Second thermonuclear detonation: 1.2 megatons, September 8, 1968. Billaud oversaw the event.

CHINA

China's new communist leadership saw the United States, which supported Chiang Kai-Party shek's in Taiwan, as its greatest foreign threat after winning the civil war in 1949. Since the Korean War (1950–53), China has grown increasingly concerned about American military action, including the possibility of nuclear reprisal against its people and land.

When Mao Zedong and the Chinese leadership decided to construct their own nuclear weapons on January 15, 1955, as a result of the Cold War, 1955 to 1958, China relied on Russian scientific and technological aid, but by 1958 the Chinese had become more self-sufficient. China, along with the other nuclear-armed governments, began the massive mobilization of manpower and resources required.

Gansu Province's Lanzhou Gaseous Diffusion Plant (LGDP) and Jiuquan Atomic Energy Complex (JAEC) are among the world's first large-scale uranium and plutonium production/processing facilities. Both the JAEC reactor and a large-scale reprocessing facility come online at the same time in April 1970, after they were both completed in 1967. Nine Academies, a design lab in Haiyan, Qinghai province, was formed and the first batch of products were made to be found east of the Koko Nor (Blue Lake). In October of that year, work began on a test site in the far northern Chinese province of Lop Nur. Nuclear weapons research was overseen by Wang Ganchang, Zhu Guangya and the other heads of the Chinese nuclear program: Deng Jiaxian, Zhou Guangzhao, Yu Min, and Chen Nengkuan. In his role as head of the State Science and Technology Commission, Marshal Nie Rongzhen guided and led the organization from 1958 to 1967. As part of Mao Zedong's "Third Line" project, a more advanced nuclear complex was built in the 1970s and 1980 to complement and eventually replace the original nuclear facilities in remote areas of China in the case of a conflict.

In contrast to the early American, Soviet, and British tests, Chinese scientists used uranium-235 in a 20-kiloton implosion design on October 16, 1964. Following that, designs for plutonium were developed. The PRC conducted 23 air tests and 22 underground tests between 1964 and 1996. Faulty testing led to a wide range of fission and fusion bomb designs, with outputs that might go up to several megatons, depending on the specific design's output capability.

The development of atomic weapons coincided with the start of China's study into thermonuclear weapons' effectiveness. An experimental group was formed in December 1960 by the Institute of Atomic Energy in order to study thermonuclear materials and reactions. For thermonuclear physics research, Deng Jiaxian's Theoretical Department at China's ninth academy was given the responsibility of shifting to nuclear design after the atomic bomb was completed in late 1963. Lithium-6 deuteride production facilities have been constructed, as well as other necessary components.

The development of a multi-stage bomb began in 1965 and was completed in 1966, with a test device ready by the end of 1967. Chinese scientists detonated the first multistage fusion device with a yield of three megatons on June 17, 1967, only 32 months after the country conducted its first atomic test, the shortest time interval among the world's initial five nuclear powers..

INDIA

India's nuclear policies and initiatives are unique when compared to those of other nuclear countries, and they were divided into three separate eras between 1947 and 1998: Originally proposed by Indian Prime Minister Jawaharlal Nehru in 1948, the

Atomic Energy Act was signed into law the following year. With Homi Bhabha serving as its chairperson, the Atomic Energy Commission (AEC) was created as a result of the act. To help design India's nuclear program, Bhabha used his Cambridge-educated background in physics as his secretary for the Department of Atomic Energy in 1954.

A pioneer in the field, Bhabha was the first person from India to hold this post. In December 1953, President Dwight D. Eisenhower made his Atoms for Peace speech at the United Nations. A main goal of the program was to prevent the proliferation of nuclear weapons by offering technology for civilian use in exchange for a guarantee not to use it for weapons systems." The objective failed owing to the dual applications of atomic energy, which is despite the fact that atomic energy is inherent in the technologies. In spite of the fact that this was discovered at the beginning of the nuclear era, it wasn't acknowledged at the time of its conception:

To help India's nuclear program in 1955, Canada offered to build a heavy water research reactor, which would use some heavy water supplied by the US. Near Bombay (Mumbai), India's principal nuclear weapons production facility, a nuclear reactor was built. After Bhabha's death in 1966, it was renamed the Bhabha Atomic Research Centre [BARC]. In order to salvage plutonium from spent nuclear fuel rods, a reprocessing plant was built nearby Using the PUREX (plutonium-uranium-extraction) chemical technique developed in the United States and made public as part of the Atoms for Peace program, the plant manufactured nuclear weapons.

Hundreds of Indian scientists and engineers have received nuclear technology training from the United States in laboratories and universities around the country. India built its first plutonium bomb In 1964. Even though military research continued over the next decade, it was complemented by work on non-military uses of nuclear energy. Although India refused to sign the Nuclear Non-Proliferation Treaty of 1968,

On May 18, 1974, a nuclear weapon with a yield of less than 5 kilotons exploded in Pokhran, Rajasthan, India. (At the time, India said 12 kilotons.) India declared the underground test as harmless, with no aspirations to create nuclear weapons. Among the important scientists and engineers involved were Homi Sethna, chairman of the AEC, Raja Ramanna, head of the BARC physics group, and Rajagopala Chidambaram, who designed the plutonium core. Chidambaram became AEC Chairman in 1998 and oversaw the tests described below. Others listed were P.K. Iyengar, Satinder K. Sikka, Pranab R. Dastidar, Sekharipuram N.A. Seshadri, and Nagapattinam S. Venkatesan.

A new phase began in 1974 and continued until 1998. However, India possessed the technical capabilities to build nuclear weapons throughout this time period. Indian officials maintained their long-standing policy of advocating nuclear disarmament but simultaneously hinting that military action was possible if necessary. During the 1980s and 1990s, Indian scientists refined nuclear designs, including theoretical work on thermonuclear weapons. Some aircraft modifications and developments in ballistic missile programs have pushed the idea of a deployed nuclear force closer, in part because Pakistan is developing its own nuclear weapons and tensions with China.

On May 11, 1998, three bombs were simultaneously exploded at the Pokhran test site in India. Fission, thermonuclear, and tactical devices were all used in the test, according to the press statement. The 0.2

kiloton tactical bomb was the most powerful. On May 13th, two more tactical devices, 0.2 and 0.6 kilotons, were exploded. They later debated over the yields' size and whether any were thermonuclear weapons. American intelligence says the second stage did not ignite. Some accounts claim one of the tests used reactor-grade plutonium. In addition to Abdul Kalam, the chairman of India's Defense Research and Development Organization, AEC chairman Rajagopala Chidambaram, BARC director Anil Kakodkar, and scientists M.S. Ramakumar, S.K. Gupta, and D.D. Sood were among the key figures in attendance at the conference.

Since 1998, India has been actively developing weapons systems for all three military services. The growing triad includes land-based ballistic missiles, air-delivered bombs, and sea-based surface-to-air missiles. India has not signed the Comprehensive Nuclear-Test-Ban Treaty, and may be obliged to test again.

PAKISTAN

By accepting an American-built research reactor that began functioning in 1965, Pakistan took advantage of the Atoms for Peace program. Despite the fact that its military nuclear development had been limited up to that time, things quickly altered. Pakistan's pursuit of the atomic bomb followed India's defeat in December 1971, which led to East Pakistan's independence as Bangladesh.

After the cease-fire, Pakistan's new president, Zulfikar Ali Bhutto, summoned his finest scientists and instructed them to build an atomic bomb. Bhutto, long distrustful of India, wished for Pakistan to have the bomb, and now had it.

"We shall eat grass and leaves if India builds the bomb, but we will get our own," he famously said. We're out of options."

Pakistan's approach to the bomb involved high-speed gas centrifuge enrichment. Professor Abdul Qadeer Khan, a Pakistani scientist educated at the University of Liege in Belgium, was a key figure. In May 1972, he joined URENCO's Dutch partner Ultra Centrifuge Nederland in its Amsterdam laboratory. In 1970, the United Kingdom, West Germany, and the Netherlands formed URENCO to ensure that they had enough enriched uranium for their civilian power reactors. Within three years, Khan had access to the firm's confidential centrifuge designs at the Almelo enrichment plant in the Netherlands. After the 1974 Indian test, he addressed Bhutto. The centrifuges were designed and photographed, and Khan returned to Pakistan with the contact information for hundreds of companies that supplied the parts. Khan left his job unexpectedly in December 1975 and returned to Pakistan with the plans and photographs.

In July 1976, Khan founded the Engineering Research Laboratories to build and manage a centrifuge plant in Kahuta utilizing components from Europe and overseas. In the future, Khan would use these connections to build a large black market network that would supply nuclear technology, centrifuges, and other goods to North Korea. For some or all of these transactions, Khan would have needed the knowledge of Pakistan's authorities, military and security agencies.

Pakistan had enriched uranium and weapon-grade uranium by April 1978. Decades later, thousands of centrifuges produced enough uranium for Pakistan to build a nuclear device by 1988, according to Pakistani Army Chief Gen. Mirza Aslam Beg. Khan apparently got the warhead design from China, where he purportedly got ideas for an implosion device that used uranium instead of plutonium in an October 1966 test.

After the May 1998 Indian nuclear tests, Pakistan claimed to have successfully exploded five nuclear devices in the Ros Koh Hills, Balochistan, on May 28 and a sixth device two days later, 100 kilometers (60 miles) to the southwest. Like India's nuclear claims, outside scientists questioned the stated yields and even the number of tests. A single Western seismic measurement on May 28 reported a yield of 9-12 kilotons, lower than Pakistan's 40-45 kilotons. Official Pakistani estimates of the May 30 nuclear test ranged from 15 to 18 kilotons. But Pakistan had joined the nuclear club and was in an arms race with India, as evidenced by its several ballistic and cruise missile programmes.

ISRAEL

Israel obtained nuclear weapons, albeit it has never admitted it. "Israel will not be the first state to introduce nuclear weapons into the region," said Prime Minister Levi Eshkol in the mid-1960s.

Israel began its nuclear program in the 1950s. It has three key figures. First Israeli Prime Minister David Ben-Gurion pursued nuclear weapons development.

Shimon Peres, director-general of the Ministry of Defense, selected employees and allocated resources behind the scenes. Ernst David Bergmann, the first chairman of Israel's Atomic Energy Commission, provided early technical guidance.

Israel's prosperity relied on France's cooperation. In October 1957, France agreed to sell Israel a reactor and an underground reprocessing plant in Dimona in the Negev desert. Many Israeli scientists and engineers trained in French nuclear power reactors. Oslo pledged to provide the reactor 20 metric tons of heavy water through the UK in 1959.

After the project was weaponized, the Ministry of Defense founded RAFAEL (Armaments Development Authority) and the Dimona Nuclear Research Centre (Negev). Dimona began construction in late 1958 or early 1959. As of the eve of the June 1967 Six-Day War (see Arab-Israeli conflicts), Israel had two or three plutonium bombs built. The Dimona plant's plutonium production has increased over time. Israel's nuclear program is said to have benefited from the work of scientists like Jenka Ratner and Avraham Hermoni.

More information about Israel's nuclear program and arsenal has been available thanks to Mordechai

Vanunu, a Dimona technician from 1977 until 1985. Before leaving his post, Vanunu took dozens of images of Dimona's most secret places, plutonium components, a full-scale thermonuclear bomb model, and work on tritium that proved Israel had created advanced weapons.. A piece headlined "Inside Dimona, Israel's Nuclear Bomb Factory" appeared in the London Sunday Times on October 5, 1986, describing his knowledge in detail. Five days before the article was published, the Mossad kidnapped Vanunu in Rome, tried him, and sentenced him to 18 years in prison. During his ten-year term, he was solitary.

They determined that Israel's nuclear arsenal was larger than previously assumed (between 100 and 200 warheads) and that Israel could develop a neutron bomb (low-yield thermonuclear device that maximizes radiation effect) from the images they had taken. (Israel may have tested a nuclear device over the Indian Ocean on September 22, 1979.) The US Defence Intelligence Agency estimates Israel possessed 60-80 nuclear weapons around the turn of the century.

SOUTH AFRICA

South Africa is the only country that has made nuclear weapons and then taken them apart and thrown them away. De Klerk told the South African parliament on March 24, 1993, that the government had built six nuclear devices and then destroyed them before signing the Nuclear Non-Proliferation Treaty on July 10, 1991.

Initially intended for peaceful purposes, South Africa decided to develop nuclear explosive capabilities in 1974. However, the program swiftly morphed into a military program in response to growing concerns about communist expansion on the country's frontiers after 1977.

 Despite the fact that over 1,000 people worked on different parts of the weapon program, only a few people knew all of the details. J.W. de Villiers is thought to have been in charge of making the explosive. The Y-Plant at Valindaba, which is near the Pelindaba Nuclear Research Center, made the first batch of highly enriched uranium in 1978. It is 19 kilometers (12 miles) west of Pretoria. South African scientists came up with a "aerodynamic" way to get more uranium. In this method, uranium hexafluoride and hydrogen gas are compressed and sent into tubes that are spun to separate the isotopes.

A design for a fission cannon assembly was chosen that looked a lot like the Little Boy bomb that was dropped on Hiroshima, so it was chosen. In the South African version, 55 kg of highly enriched uranium was supposed to be inside, and it was supposed to have a yield of 10 to 18 kilotons, or about 55 pounds.

They made seven weapons in 1985. At the end of 1989, when the government stopped making them, six had been finished and the seventh was in the early stages of building. Nuclear and non-nuclear parts were kept apart in the storage facility.

Each weapon had two pieces of highly enriched uranium that were not critical. They were kept in vaults in the Kentron Circle complex, which was later called Advena. It was about 16 kilometers (10 miles) east of Pelindaba, where the weapons were built. The weapon weighed about a ton, was about 6 feet long, and had a diameter of about 63.5 cm (25 inches) when fully built.

This might have been supplied by a customized Buccaneer missile. There were no plans to use the bombs in an offensive way, and they were never part of the armed forces.

Dismantled: The uranium was turned into something that could not be used for weapons, the parts and technical records were destroyed, and the Y-Plant was shut down over the next 18 months after the government decided to stop arming itself, The International Atomic Energy Agency (IAEA) started visiting South Africa's facilities in November 1991. They found that the weapons program had been stopped and the devices had been removed from the country's facilities.

South African officials say that the weapons were never meant to be used in the military. Instead, they were meant to make Western governments, especially the United States, come to South Africa's aid if the country was in danger. South Africa was supposed to be the first country to tell the West that it had a bomb. If that doesn't work, South Africa will either openly say that it has nuclear weapons or detonate a nuclear weapon in a deep hole at the Vastrap test site in the Kalahari to show that it has them.

NORTH KOREA

Few reliable facts about North Korea's nuclear development have been made public so far. Most of what we know comes from Western intelligence agencies and academics, but not all of it. Fear that the US might use nuclear weapons during and after the Korean War may have led North Korean leader Kim Il-sung to start working on his own nuclear weapons in the 1960s. The Soviet Union helped with this project as well. Over the next two decades, China helped with different things. Pakistani uranium enrichment technology and warhead designs were said to have been given to Pakistan by Abdul Qadeer Khan.

There is a place called Yngbyn about 60 miles north of Pyongyang that is the heart of North Korea's nuclear weapons project. A reactor that started working in 1986, a reprocessing plant, and a plant that makes fuel are some of the main places. People who live near a 5-megawatt reactor can make about 6 kg (13 pounds) of plutonium a year there. One or two weapons made with plutonium made before 1992 were almost ready for use in early 1990s, according to the US Central Intelligence Agency.

As a result of a deal between the United States and North Korea, North Korea's nuclear program was almost completely stopped from 1994 to 2002. The deal shut down North Korea's nuclear reactor. According to the United States, North Korea had resumed its military nuclear program in October

2002. In response, Pyongyang announced its withdrawal from the Nuclear Nonproliferation Treaty, becoming the first nation to do so. The reactor in North Korea has been running again, and more plutonium has been found.

Estimates of how much plutonium was separated and how many bombs were made from it aren't the same. The amount of plutonium that was made for weapons was between 28 and 50 kg (62 and 110 pounds). For 5 to 12 weapons that each weighed 4 to 5 kg, this would be enough (9 to 11 pounds). It all depended on how good North Korean designers were at making things work and how much they wanted their weapons to make.

North Korea did an underground nuclear test in the northeastern Hamgyng Mountains on October 9, 2006, to see if it could make a bomb. Western scientists think the yield was about one kiloton, which is a lot less than other countries' first nuclear tests. It was claimed by Chinese government officials that Pyongyang had told them ahead of time that a four-kiloton test was going to be done. In the next year, the US and other countries in the region tried to stop North Korea from making nuclear weapons. They used international pressure and focused diplomacy.

Other countries don't speak the same language as us

After World War II, many countries started working on nuclear research and development projects. For different reasons, they didn't go any further and start making real nuclear weapons, though. Sweden, for example, ran a nuclear weapons research program for 20 years, from the late 1940s to the late 1960s. Then, the government decided not to go any further. Switzerland also looked into the idea, but didn't go very far with it either.

The term "virtual nuclear country" is still used in some places, like Japan and Germany, because they have the technical know-how and separate plutonium at home that they can use to make a weapon quickly.

Several more countries had plans to build nuclear weapons that were put on hold because of outside pressure, a friendship with an enemy, or their own decisions not to build them. Taiwan, Argentina, Brazil, Libya, and Iraq are all examples of this type of place. This material could be used to make nuclear bombs, even though the International Atomic Energy Agency and the United Nations Security Council warned that it could be used to make nuclear bombs. Iran now has the ability to make enriched uranium. Those programs for each country are explained one by one in the text below.

TAIWAN

Though a few facts have come to light, the goal and scope of Taiwan's project are still unknown. After China did a nuclear test in 1964, Taiwan started making weapon-grade nuclear material. It got a small research reactor from Canada and other facilities from other countries. After years of pressure from the United States and the International Atomic Energy Agency, Taiwan finally agreed to give up its nuclear program.

Argentina and Brazil are two countries that are bordered by each other on one side.

Argentina and Brazil were engaged in a competitive nuclear weapons development program in the late 1970s and early 1980s, which was substantially funded by their respective military regimes at the time. In the early 1990s, both countries agreed to cease their nuclear weapons programs, submit to inspections, and join the Nuclear Nonproliferation Treaty, effectively putting an end to the competition.

LIBYA

Libya began developing a clandestine nuclear weapons program in the early 1980s, in violation of its international treaty commitments under the Nuclear Nonproliferation Treaty. Despite the fact that just a small number of centrifuges were finished and placed into service, Libya's nuclear program expanded after the year 2000, when the country began importing parts for 10,000 centrifuges to enrich uranium.

It was in October 2003 that the US Navy captured and diverted a German freighter bound for Tripoli that was transporting thousands of centrifuge components that had originated from Abdul Qadeer Khan's black market network.

During a public speech in December 2003, Libyan leader Muammar al-Qaddafi stated that all weapons of mass destruction (WMD) projects would be terminated and that inspectors would be permitted to verify their destruction. In spite of the fact that the nuclear warhead would have been too large to fit on a Libyan missile, Libyan authorities claimed to have obtained designs for nuclear warheads from Khan in the course of their negotiations. A team of experts that investigated the Libyan program concluded that it was still in its early stages, that it was poorly managed and understaffed, and that it remained unfinished, and that it would take several years to produce an atomic weapon.

IRAQ

Although a signatory to the Nuclear Non-Proliferation Treaty, Iraq began developing a clandestine nuclear weapons program in the 1970s, claiming it was for peaceful purposes. In 1976, France agreed to sell Iraq an Osirak or Tammuz-1 research reactor, which used weapon-grade uranium as fuel.

The reactor was completed in 1977. Iraq purchased hundreds of tons of uranium from countries such as Portugal, Niger, and Brazil, as well as sending a large number of professionals overseas for training. In 1979, Iraq negotiated an agreement with Italians to acquire a plutonium extraction plant. On June 7, 1981, Israeli bombers bombed the Osirak nuclear reactor in Iraq, destroying the reactor's core and putting an end to the country's nuclear weapons program. Through the next decade, Iraq attempted numerous methods of uranium enrichment, but its lofty objectives were never achieved, and only a few grams of weapon-grade nuclear material had been produced by the end of the Persian Gulf War (1990–91). United Nations inspectors found a large-scale Iraqi clandestine biological weapons program after President Saddam Hussein's son-in-law Hussein Kamil fled to the United States in August 1995. In 1998, Saddam Hussein dismissed United Nations inspectors, sparking suspicions that nuclear weapons developments were being pursued once more.

The inspectors returned in November 2002, but they discovered no evidence of restarted programs before the Iraq War began on March 20, 2003, according to the inspectors. No weapons of mass destruction were discovered in Iraq when the United States invaded the country in 2003 and 2004.

IRAN

The United States received intelligence in the late 1970s that Mohammad Reza Shah Pahlavi had developed a clandestine nuclear weapons program despite the fact that he signed the Nuclear Non-Proliferation Treaty in 1968. Despite the fact that the program was put on hold by the Islamic Revolution of 1979 and the ensuing Iran-Iraq War (1980–88), new attempts were underway by the late 1980s, aided by Abdul Qadeer Khan, who gave Iran gas centrifuge technology and taught Iranian scientists and engineers.

Furthermore, Iran began secretly constructing a number of nuclear facilities in violation of the International Atomic Energy Agency's safeguards agreements. An Iranian opposition group based in Paris raised concerns about the presence of a uranium enrichment plant at Naanz and a heavy water reactor at Ark in 2002, prompting the International Atomic Energy Agency (IAEA) to intervene.

International suspicions were aroused when Iran signed a contract with Russia in 1995 to complete a nuclear power facility at Bshehr that had been started by West Germany in the mid-1970s, provoking international concerns that it may be used for nuclear weapons development. Inspectors from the International Atomic Energy Agency (IAEA) began examining suspicious locations in February 2003, raising questions about their purpose. In September 2005, the IAEA's Governing Board determined Iran to be in violation of its safeguards obligations. Iranian officials have stated that they are developing nuclear technologies for peaceful civilian purposes, which is permitted under the Nuclear Non-Proliferation Treaty. However, many people believe that Iran is constructing a nuclear infrastructure in order to produce a nuclear weapon at some point in the future.

By 2005, the Bshehr nuclear power plant was nearly completed. Iran had produced enough low-enriched uranium (less than 5 percent uranium-235) at its enrichment facility by 2008 to power a single implosion-type fission weapon—if the low-enriched uranium was further enriched to around 90 percent uranium-235.

This was in addition to the new reactor fuel supplied by Russia at the time. However, enrichment of uranium-235 beyond 5 percent would be a violation of Iran's safeguards commitments, and the enrichment process would almost probably be detected by IAEA inspectors before the highly enriched uranium could be used to build a nuclear weapon with a high probability of success. A final deal was reached in July 2015 between Iran and the P5+1 group of international powers, which included the United States, China, Russia, France, Germany, and the United Kingdom. The accord limits Iran's nuclear program. As a condition for the restoration of sanctions, Iran pledged to dramatically reduce its nuclear stockpile and let inspectors from the International Atomic Energy Agency access to its nuclear sites. The consequences were in place since January 2016.